I0053383

AMAZON FBA

Proven Step by Step Strategies to Make Money on Amazon

Mark Smith

© Copyright 2016 by Mark Smith - All rights reserved.

This document is geared towards providing exact and reliable information in regards to the topic and issue covered. The publication is sold with the idea that the publisher is not required to render accounting, officially permitted, or otherwise, qualified services. If advice is necessary, legal or professional, a practiced individual in the profession should be ordered.

- From a Declaration of Principles which was accepted and approved equally by a Committee of the American Bar Association and a Committee of Publishers and Associations.

In no way is it legal to reproduce, duplicate, or transmit any part of this document in either electronic means or in printed format. Recording of this publication is strictly prohibited and any storage of this document is not allowed unless with written permission from the publisher. All rights reserved.

The information provided herein is stated to be truthful and consistent, in that any liability, in terms of inattention or otherwise, by any usage or abuse of any policies, processes, or directions contained within is the solitary and utter responsibility of the recipient reader. Under no circumstances will any legal responsibility or blame be held against the publisher for any reparation, damages, or monetary loss due to the information herein, either directly or indirectly.

Respective authors own all copyrights not held by the publisher.

The information herein is offered for informational purposes solely, and is universal as so. The presentation of the information is without contract or any type of guarantee assurance.

The trademarks that are used are without any consent, and the publication of the trademark is without permission or backing by the trademark owner. All trademarks and brands within this book are for clarifying purposes only and are the owned by the owners themselves, not affiliated with this document.

Table of Contents

Introduction 5

Chapter 1: Selling On Amazon 6

    Some Tips 11

Chapter 2: Fulfillment by Amazon................................14

    Different Types of Sellers 16

Chapter 3: Benefits of FBA..19

    Grow Your Business 19

    Costs Less 21

    Customer Service...22

    Cash on Delivery...23

    Prime Eligibility..23

    Buy Box..25

Chapter 4: Being an FBA Seller....................................26

    Find a Product 26

    Making an Account...28

    Tools...29

Chapter 5: Details of FBA..31

    Costs...31

    Labeling 32

    Product 33

Chapter 6: The Procedure 35

Conclusion...40

Introduction

I want to thank you and congratulate you for choosing this book, Amazon FBA for beginners.

This book contains proven steps and strategies on how to start your Amazon FBA experience. Selling on Amazon through FBA can be a life changing experience. It makes business so easy and simplified that you would have enough time for work and for yourself.

Amazon provides various benefits to anyone who wants to get into the FBA business. You won't find these anywhere else because in essence, Amazon does all the work for you. You also get the opportunity to market yourself to the millions of users that Amazon has.

For a seller in 2016, getting in on the Amazon FBA experience is very important in order expand your business and to learn more about selling online. It's also hassle free. Amazon provides you with step-by-step instructions on how to be a fully-fledged FBA seller. Your only job is to focus on creating innovative products for your customers.

This book will tell you everything you need to know on starting your business with Amazon. I have tried to simplify the procedure so that you are able to understand the basics. There are also numerous tips mentioned throughout this book that will make you an expert in the FBA field.

Without much ado, lets get started!

Thanks again for purchasing this book, I hope you enjoy it!

Chapter 1: Selling On Amazon

In order to understand how FBA works, you have to understand how selling on Amazon works. Amazon has millions of users and is increasing its user base every day. Many people have made a lot of money working through Amazon while others are still struggling. It's also about understand how selling really works on Amazon.

If you want to be a seller on Amazon you have the opportunity of marketing your products in front of millions of active users. You will show up as a third party seller since you're operating your own business. If you open Amazon you will be able to see the list of sellers that sell a particular product. So, it's not just you who is selling the product but tons of people. The customer now has the opportunity to select from all of these sellers.

Amazon allows you to work on a larger scale without going to the trouble of establishing a shop, workers, etc. You can work on whatever scale you want. If you want to sell multiple products then you can do that but if you want to only sell a few products then that's also your choice. If you are simply trying to sell something on the Internet then there might be an issue of scale ability. You might not be able to increase your business on every website. You can function as an independent small seller who is trying to make a little bit of money. It's easy but you don't really get to function as a proper business.

That's what's different about Amazon. It gives you the opportunity to work as an independent small seller dealing only one product or you can be a business tycoon who is handing multiple products through Amazon. This is why selling on Amazon is easy. You don't need huge investments in order to get your business started. If you believe that your product will sell then you can increase the manufacturing. It's extremely risk free. You get the opportunity of making a lot of money without investing a lot. This reduces the risk factor and also helps you to be stress free.

Process

The process of selling on Amazon is easy. Amazon doesn't require much from you. They just need your bank account details and tax information. There will of course be some money that you to pay in order to start your own seller channel but Amazon has some great offers and incentives for new sellers.

Step 1: The first step is to setup your own store on Amazon. You have to register yourself and then you will be required to give a list of the products that you are selling. It's very easy and Amazon provides you with a unique tool that is easy to understand.

Make sure that you do not give any false information and the products that you are listing actually exist. This is the first step in starting your own Amazon business so you should be very careful.

Amazon also has various professional service providers that can help you in creating a unique impression for your product. This is important because you might not know how to really market your product. These professional service providers have been working for years on this kind of stuff and hence, they know the requirements of the market. They will also be able to guide you on how the procedure works. So, it's necessary for anyone who wants to sell their product on Amazon to use the help of such service providers to make sure that you can compete with the world-class sellers.

Amazon also helps you to advertise your products. Amazon's advertisements rules are brilliant. The cost of advertisements through other channels is really high. Amazon only asks for money when someone actually clicks on your advertisement. This is beneficial because you don't have to pay too much. You only have to pay for the real users.

Step 2: The second step is interacting with the customers. It will take some time for your store to go live but when it does you will be able to instantly see the results. Amazon has a collective user base of over one fifty million people just in North America. Globally, there are way too many people who use Amazon daily.

This puts you at an interesting position. You have the option of marketing your product to all of these users without the commitment that is required. You are doing it all online and if it doesn't work out, you would hardly have to deal with loss. This is the best part about Amazon. It's like joining an already built marketplace without investing a lot of money.

If you receive an order from a customer, you will be able to manage it yourself. You will be able to contact the customer if that is what you want or any other information that you might want. It's really easy to understand and the order management dashboard will help you out in whatever you need.

To create a lasting impression on your customers, it's recommended to supply them with high quality products and to also keep focusing on doing it as efficiently as possible.

Step 3: Step 3 is where Amazon makes your life easier. Amazon delivers the product for you. You don't have to do anything at all. Everything is to be dealt by Amazon representatives. You just have to simply supply Amazon with the product and once you are done, the package will be supplied through Amazon and its courier partners. Amazon will come to you in order to pick up the product. The packaging and other logistical stuff is all you have to do.

The shipping by Amazon is really fast and it's also hassle free. This will ensure that you do not lose a potential customer. You will be able to easily get your product to your customer and without any problems. If there is any issue then you can call Amazon at any point and they will resolve the issue for you. If something happens to the product while being transported then it is Amazon that takes the complete responsibility. You can put your complete trust on Amazon.

This is also where the whole FBA business comes in. Instead of just having Amazon pick the product from you, you are given the option of storing your product with Amazon. We'll have a lot of discussion on this later but essentially fulfillment by Amazon aims at reducing your workload. You have to ship the products just once to the Amazon storing facility and they'll keep the product safe for you. Once you get an order, you can direct the Amazon storing facility to ship out your order. You don't have to pack and you don't have to worry about inventory. It makes everything much easier.

This is important because it helps you to focus on your business. You can grow your business and add more product lines while Amazon deals with shipping and other charges. Amazon only takes a little money from you. You don't have to do much. Just sit back and relax.

A lot of businesses have been successful because they have been able to focus on providing customer service without getting distracted by distribution channels. It's essential in the twenty first century because it makes like easier for you. You can dedicate your time on more important things. It helps you to scale your business. If you want to expand your business then you will face the problem of shipping out the products. This can make life very difficult for someone who is handling the business alone. Fulfillment by Amazon ensures that you never have to waste your time with the shipping and packaging business. This allows you to expand your business without putting too much pressure on yourself.

Step 4: Amazon is very prompt with payments. They are an international organization and hence, you won't ever have to deal with payment problems. They deposit the payment in your bank within seven days. The fees that Amazon charges is fair and nominal. They only take fees from you if you make a sale, so they are not exploitative.

Step 5: You can use Amazon to grow your business. Amazon doesn't just ship and sell products for you. It also helps you to be a better businessman or businesswoman. It ensures that you get regular updates about your performance so that you are able to track your progress. Amazon also keeps giving you tips on how to run your business. This will help you to increase your sales and you will be able to make a lot of profits.

It also provides you with regular updates and reports. You will be able to study your performance and see your results. This makes life much easier since you don't have to get any external reporter to make these reports for you. You also don't have to deal with accounting and similar complex activities. You can scale your business as you want and Amazon will be there to help you out.

Amazon is also great for seller services. You can contact them with any query that you have at any point of time without any trouble. It will make everything much easier. You will be able to boost your performance and increase your sales.

Step 6: You can also go global with Amazon. If you wish to expand your business and sell in other countries, you can do so with Amazon. It's really difficult to sell anything overseas. To set up shop in another country and sell your products takes a lot of time and dedication. There are many permits and regional connections that you need. It's almost impossible for an individual seller to sell something abroad without investing in more resources.

Amazon on the other hand helps you to go global without any hassle. You don't need to have regional connections or permits. You can sell online through Amazon and the shipping and other miscellaneous expenses will be handled by Amazon. It's the best way of marketing your products abroad. You get the option of selling on a widely trusted platform and you don't have to invest in anything. You can go global without even getting out of your chair.

Some Tips

If you want to be really good at selling on Amazon then there are certain tips that you have to follow. The main point is to treat selling seriously. You have to innovate and research about everything that you are selling. Think ten times before you decide to sell a product and consider everything related to it from costs to reviews before you decide to sell it. Amazon changes every day and you have to stay on top of the game in order to be successful.

1. If you want to scale your business then you have to use fulfillment. If you were going to spend all of your time on packaging and shipping then you wouldn't have to time to manufacture or find the products that you want to sell. The less you sell the less profits you make. So, if you want to actually make some money through selling, scaling is inevitable. If

Amazon handles the shipping and packaging for you, it'll save enough time for you to just focus on marketing your products.

2. You have to be flexible. Don't just pick a few products to sell and go after them. If a product isn't selling them dump it and move on. You will make a lot of mistakes and incur many losses before you become an expert. If you are not willing to change then you will continue to incur losses. If you see that there are losses in selling a product then stay away from it. You have to make sure that every sale gets you some profit. Be willing to learn. There are numerous experts in the online selling business that are ready to provide you with their services. Take their help without any hesitation. They will tell you all about the new services that are present on Amazon and how you can benefit from them.

3. Manage your inventory. Make sure that everything is noted. Run it like a proper business, even if you are doing it by yourself. You do not want to lose track of your products or money. Take a note of everything and make sure that your inventory is never low. If a customer can't buy your product then you have lost them forever. Keep sending products to Amazon as soon as they are sold. Take care of your cash flow as well. You don't have to hire an accountant but make sure that you don't lose track of the money. Keep tabs on your spending and make sure it all goes as planned. People usually tend to spend way more than they should have. This can create problems while calculating profit margins. Make sure everything goes as planned.

4. If you're not doing well as soon when you started then don't freak out. It's okay to not make huge profits as soon as you start. You have to measure your progress but don't do it too often. Rather work on increasing your sales rather than profits at first. If you have to check your progress weekly then measure

it through sales. Look at the profit and the money on a quarterly or half yearly basis.

Keep your focus on making money. Don't get overwhelmed and focus on the sale that is ahead of you. Try to make as much money as you can on every sale and you will see your progress every time that you check your reports. If you really want to see huge changes then check your progress only after a certain period of time. Don't lose hope and try to innovate as much as possible.

Chapter 2: Fulfillment by Amazon

Fulfillment by Amazon (FBA) is a sales technique. It's the way that Amazon recruits more people to sell their products on its website. The main purpose behind FBA is to give people the opportunity to increase their sales without adding too much pressure on them. You can store your products at the Amazon storing facility and they will send out the product for you. All you have to do is package the product and send it to the storage facility. Then, as soon as a sale takes place, Amazon will send out the product to the required destination and you will be able to receive the money. It has a lot of benefits and most of all it gives you freedom. You can work on growing your business while Amazon deals with the shipping business for you.

FBA does not just stop at shipping. Amazon also provides customer service for you. If there is any problem with the product then you don't have to keep your phone with you at all times. Amazon will deal with the customer for you. This definitely makes selling very easy. For someone who does not have a lot of time and is doing this on the side, FBA is a lifesaver. You can earn some extra money and it doesn't even take a lot of time. It hardly requires any commitment or investment. The benefits of FBA are incalculable.

If you join FBA it also increases the strength of your product. People trust those products that are fulfilled by Amazon. So, the chances of you making a sale also increase. You will be able to sell your products easily and will be able to boost your performance. FBA sellers also get the option of delivering their products in one day. This is very important because a lot of customers buy products from Amazon just for the one-day delivery guarantee. If your product does not come under FBA then the customer won't be able to opt for the one-day delivery option.

Free Delivery is also another feature that comes under FBA. Most customers would never pay delivery charges for a product. FBA sellers get the option of free delivery on all of their products. This makes it easier for your customers to buy the product and get it delivered. The lower the cost of the product, the happier it makes the customers.

It's also been found that most sellers who join the FBA scheme tend to see an increase in their sales. The reason behind this is the aura that FBA has on your products. Most customers are hesitant in buying stuff from online retail stores. If they see that Amazon has fulfilled a product then they are more likely to buy it. It also helps you to establish credibility as a seller. On a site where there are thousands of sellers who are using FBA, if you do not use FBA then there is a pretty good chance you will be lagging behind. To ensure that you are able to deal with the competition, you have to get on FBA right now.

Amazon has world-class resources. There fulfillment centers would be able to take much better care of the products than any other storing facility. They keep the inventory with them so that you don't have to. They also pack the product for you and then ship it. This saves a lot of time for you. Amazon also ensures that their shipping and packaging service are the best in the world. This way, your customers won't have anything to complain about.

Amazon also has a great customer service network. Their representatives are present all over the world and they deal with all kinds of problems. They also provide you with regular feedbacks so that you can change your business strategy accordingly.

Different Types of Sellers

You can sell on Amazon as part of the FBA scheme or as a Merchant Fulfilled Seller (MF). It depends upon you what you want to pick but FBA is what most people recommend. The differences arise in terms of the responsibilities that you will have and the amount of work that you have to do.

If you want to be a MF seller then you have to deal with everything yourself. You won't get help from Amazon in terms of shipping and packaging. You pick a product and it goes live on the website. The customer would not see a fulfilled by Amazon tag with your product and they wouldn't be able to avail one-day delivery either. This is one of the biggest disadvantages that comes with MF. This definitely affects your performance. A lot of customers tend to not have a lot of confidence in products that are not fulfilled by Amazon.

If the customer does decide to buy your product then you will be notified by Amazon to ship the product. You have to take out time from your work to package the product. Once you have done that, you have to purchase the shipping label and post it on the package. Then, you have to personally go to the post office and ship the product to the customer. All of this takes a lot of time and patience. If you have multiple orders then it might even take a whole day to just send out a couple of products. Also, you have to make sure that the packaging is durable and the product is not harmed during transport. If it does happen then you are the one who has to answer to the customer and not Amazon.

A huge issue is shipping through post office. If you do this then you have to charge shipping charges from your customer. This increases the price of the product and there is a pretty good chance that it will lower your sales. Post offices are not exactly famous for being punctual. They might just delay the product and you wouldn't be able to do anything. It's a lot burden and there are many disadvantages associated with it. The only advantage is that you have the freedom of packaging the product as you wish and you might be able to cut down on the shipping cost. Amazon has certain quality checks that make the shipping cost increase by a margin. If you do it yourself then there is a pretty good chance that you saved some money.

But the problem is that FBA makes life so much easier that it makes no sense to be a MF seller. You don't have to package the products again and again. You just have to mail them to the Amazon storage facility and you are done. You don't have to deal with order; the storage facility does that for you. Your customers get the advantage of having one-day delivery. Your sales would definitely increase, as more people tend to buy Amazon fulfilled products than those that are not fulfilled by Amazon.

Amazon also ensures that your product reaches its destination on time. You don't have to worry about your product getting lost and you don't have to directly deal with the customer. You get so much time to grow your business and boost your performance that you will surely recommend FBA to others.

Your product is also featured as a Prime eligible purchase. It means that the customer can pick a better delivery system and get the product faster. It's mostly two days and this ensures that the customer is absolutely happy with the purchase.

You have to pay some part of your sales to Amazon for storing the product and handling the shipping for you. You can also sell as many products as you want because you are not the one who has to worry about packing, processing and shipping. You can scale your business to a huge size without any worries.

Scaling is important because if you list more items for sale, the more money you make. Now, if you are the one who has to deal with packing and shipping then you won't want to scale. It puts too much pressure on you since you can't handle the amount of orders that are coming in. If there is even a little delay then the customer would be unhappy and you might even lose money. You can sell as many products as you want on Amazon because that is your main job. You just have to deal with finding better products to sell on Amazon without wasting your time on the packaging. If there are too many orders then it's the Amazon storage facility, which has to deal with the intake and not you.

You also get a place to store your products. You don't have to worry about maintaining inventory and taking care of it. Amazon hardly charges you for inventory; rather it just takes a part of your sales and only charges for shipping and handling. This saves a lot of time and money.

Chapter 3: Benefits of FBA

FBA has many obvious benefits. If you want to really increase your sales and give a boost to your business then FBA is the way to go. The main benefit is related to how much time you save. You don't have to spend days packaging and shipping products. This makes your business much more efficient.

Amazon has a lot of expertise in the customer satisfaction department and they know what they are doing. If you decide to use their services then you will benefit from their expertise. You just have to pack and they ship it for you. They even handle the returns on the product for you. They take the complaints from customers and forward them to you. They run a virtual business to help you sell more and more while only charging nominal fees.

Grow Your Business

A lot of people want to grow their business and make it better but they can't. They don't have the time and patience for it. It's usually because handling everything yourself can be really difficult. If you are someone who sells products on the Internet then you will have a lot of problem. You would have to handle the logistics of all of your products. Creating product listings and writing out details takes a lot of time. If you have to handle sales along with this then that completely takes all of your time. So, if you have the added pressure of packing and shipping the products to customers then you cannot hope to grow your business.

Amazon allows you to focus on your business so that you don't have to get into the small things. You don't have to waste your time with packing and shipping. You just have to do it once. Just ship everything to the Amazon storing facility and your job is done. If there is an order, the storage facility workers will find your product. Package it and then ship it. They will ensure that the product reaches its destination on time. This gives you the opportunity to expand your business without any boundaries. You don't have to be constrained by anything at all.

Building Trust

Amazon is a huge organization that has existed for many years. Every customer that wants to buy something on Amazon trusts that the product he will receive would be of brilliant quality. Amazon helps in building trust between the customer and the seller.

The FBA sign on your product increases the value of your product. People are more likely to buy a product if they see this sign. There are thousands of sellers on Amazon and it becomes really difficult for the customer to pick just one. The one thing that a customer does know is that they can trust Amazon. So, if they see that Amazon has fulfilled a product they trust the seller.

This is very important to increase your sales. At a place where you can't have any actual contact with the customers, your product page is what determines a sale. So, in order to ensure that a sale happens you have to use the goodwill that is associated with the Amazon brand name.

All Amazon customers trust that Amazon will provide them with high quality services. They trust that the product will be brilliant and they will get it on time. If you have the FBA sign on your product then this trust is automatically transferred to your product.

It's also a fact that Amazon fulfilled products are easier to return since it is Amazon that deals with returns for FBA sellers. This also induces customers to pick FBA sellers instead of non-FBA ones. Amazon also provides the opportunity to be your customer care representative. If a customer has a problem, he can simply call Amazon for help. This way Amazon handles the customers for you.

Costs Less

Amazon ensures that you only pay for the services that you use. You don't have to pay a certain sum to start with FBA. The charges aren't fixed but rather depend on your usage. If you do not use a certain service in a particular month then you don't have to pay for it.

The charges are really flexible. If you use a service only a few times then you pay for the times that you actually used the service. There is also no subscription fee. You can join the FBA scheme without paying anything at all.

Another amazing thing about FBA is that there are no minimum unit requirements. You can ship as many units as you want to the storage facility. You don't have to deal with any pressure with respect to manufacturing.

Amazon even provides you with the option of advertising your product through the site. You only pay for an advertisement if people actually visit your product through it. If nobody looks at the advertisement and you don't get any hit on your product through it, you don't have to pay at all.

Amazon is really great when it comes to pricing. They don't charge for unnecessary services and they don't have any hidden costs. They tell you from the starting what they are going to charge.

When you're sending your product to Amazon storage facility, you don't have to spend a lot of money since Amazon service providers pick the products from your doorstep. You can also pick to send the product to their storage facility by using your own courier service.

Amazon also takes its fee only if you make a sale. There are no fixed charges on Amazon. Amazon only charges some fees if you are making some money. If you are not able to sell anything then Amazon won't charge anything from you.

Customer Service

Amazon handles customers for you. It gives you a space to sell your product so that you can market to millions of customers. It also handles customer service for you.

If you are not selling through FBA, Amazon would take the customer service calls but you would be the one who has to deal with the problems that the customer has. If the customer hasn't received the product then you have to ensure that the product is on time. You also have to deal with tracking. All of this can be really time consuming and painful for someone just getting into the selling business.

Through FBA, Amazon will handle all the customers for you. You won't have to ever take a phone call and deal with customer related queries. Instead, you can focus on growing your business and adding more products.

Returns are really difficult to deal with. You have to deal with the customer then get the product from the customer. It further wastes time and you can't focus on the sales that you might be getting. To ensure that you do not get distracted and can continue your work, Amazon handles the returns for you. You don't have to get the product from the customer; Amazon does it. You don't even have to unpack and catalog the product again. The product goes back to the storage facility it came from and is cataloged again there. This makes your job much easier since you don't have to deal with such logistical issues.

Cash on Delivery

Cash on Delivery has been extremely popular in growing nations. Unlike other countries, these nations still aren't completely dependent on cards. Many still rely on cash and many prefer cash on delivery because of this. Other than that there is growing mistrust for online selling which is why most like to pay only when they have the product in their hand.

Amazon FBA ensures that all of your products are eligible for cash on delivery. This is not something that you can avail if you pick to be a MF seller. That's because sending a product through any postal service is risky and if you use postal service to collect cash for you, you're just playing with your luck. Amazon picks the money for you and deposits it in your account. This way you do not miss out on any customer and you do not miss out on money either.

Prime Eligibility

The best advantage that you'll receive because of FBA is that your product gets Prime eligibility.

Amazon has tried a lot to make sure that people join its Prime accounts. Prime costs a lot but people still spend money to get

Prime accounts because of the amount of benefits that they receive because of it. All of your orders are eligible for two-day delivery for free. This is a huge advantage and many customers join Amazon for this particular reason only. There are many other benefits that a Prime customer enjoys but the main one to focus on is the faster delivery options.

If you are part of the FBA scheme then all of your products are eligible for Prime. It means that all of your customers would get their products in two days. This ensures that your customers are satisfied and they keep buying. If you are a customer who wants to buy a product and you don't have the option of getting your products delivered in two days then you would obviously pick another seller.

Amazon itself ensures that people pick Prime sellers. If you look at the sellers available on Amazon then your eyes would definitely go to all those sellers that have Prime written next to them and have two-day delivery. This forces any customer to go for the Prime seller.

So, it's almost a necessity to be part of the FBA scheme if you want to retain your customers. Most customers tend to pick sellers who are FBA rather than MF even if the price is high. This is because being part of FBA adds credibility to your product and your products get delivered in two days.

Being part of FBA is a requirement and not a choice. If you want to be better than other sellers then you have to pick it. You might lose customers due to many other reasons but at least you won't lose them because you didn't deliver the product faster and in a more efficient way. FBA also ensures that you can make huge profits on all of your sales. Amazon cuts down on the excess expenses that you might have made trying to package and ship the product. This ensures that you sell your product in the best way possible.

Buy Box

A buy box is an opportunity for a seller to earn the right to be the one whose product previews if a customer clicks on it. There are various sellers for every product on Amazon, the seller that gets featured in the preview of the product is said to have the Buy Box for that particular product.

Getting a Buy Box is really difficult. Being an FBA seller increases your chances of having a Buy Box. Buy Boxes are really important because they impact your sales. Many people don't even know that there are multiple sellers for a product. They simply buy the product as soon as they open it. This gives the seller with the buy box a huge advantage.

Even though being an FBA seller is not a requirement but to be eligible for a buy box it is recommended to be an FBA seller. It's really hard to get the buy box for any product. So, if you want to get ahead of other sellers or at least be on level ground with them, you have to get FBA.

Chapter 4: Being an FBA Seller

If you think that FBA is the way to go then there are only a few steps that you have to follow in order to become an FBA Seller. You don't really have to do much. If you have a unique product that you make then you can sell it online without any hassle. Even if you don't have any product to sell, you can always use various tricks to come up with unique products. The point is that FBA is a gold mine. It doesn't matter what product you are selling. If you sell it on Amazon then you will definitely make a lot of money. Your profit margins will be huge and you wouldn't require a lot of investment.

Find a Product

If you want to be an FBA seller then you have to find the right product. This is because not all products have a huge online market. Many of them wouldn't sell online at all, like cars or expensive watches. So, you have to make sure that your product is uniquely suitable for online marketing.

You also have to make sure that the product that you pick will be beneficial for you. You have to get the product as cheap as possible so that you can sell it at full price in order to make some profit. The margin should be pretty large because you have to pay Amazon as well for its services.

Now, if you can find a product that you think is correct then great, otherwise you can always use retail products. If you want to earn some extra cash then this is simple. All you have to do is get retail products then sell them on Amazon through FBA to make huge profits. It's a tried and tested scheme. You won't have to do much but you'll still be able to make a lot of money.

The main aim is to find a retail product either offline or online. You have to find the product at its cheapest. So, make sure that you look everywhere before you buy the product.

Look for products that are at selling at discounts. This is so that you can sell the product for full on Amazon and make huge profits. There will definitely be some mall around you that has a discount going on. Look for such places and use them for your own advantage.

Try to look for products with at least 25% discount. This leaves enough room for you to jack up the price and make some nice profit. If a store is having a clearance sale or closing down then it will definitely have the products that you need.

Now, you have to use an app called Scoutify. Scoutify is a brilliant app that lists the current price of a product on Amazon. So, find a store and then go into it with the Scoutify app handy. Scan the barcode of the product with the camera on your phone and Scoutify will pull up the stats about the product. You will be able to see at what price the product is currently selling on Amazon. You will also see how many sellers are selling the product and the bestseller rank of the product. This way you can make some quick calculations to see if you will be able to sell the product on Amazon at a profit.

The main aim is find a product whose price can be increased to make a profit and still the price should be lower than what is currently selling on Amazon. So, you can make out at what cost you should buy the product and what would be your profitability on buying the product.

Now, before you get out there and start selling your products, make sure you test a few products that you have found at home. Fox example, I'll be taking a blue can opener. The aim of this exercise is to show you how to calculate the profit you will make by selling a product.

A can opener is listed at $30 on Amazon. Now, you have to use this app called Amazon FBA calculator. Just Google and you'll be able to use the app since it's free. Just input whatever the calculator wants and you will be able to see the profit that you will make if the can opener sells at this price.

The profit margin is huge on most products. The calculator told me that I could make almost $20 if the product sells. So, if I can somehow find a shop that sells this can opener at $15, I can make $5 profit. If you start looking around in stores you will find a lot of stuff that's still not on Amazon. You can sell these products at even more profits.

Making an Account

If you have finally decided that you do want to sell your product on Amazon then you can go ahead and make an account. So, go to the Amazon site and scroll to the bottom. You will find the option of 'Sell on Amazon' at the bottom left side.

Now, if you are looking to start a serious business then I recommend that you sign up as a pro seller. There are various benefits that you get if you use a pro seller account and if you do actually want to make money in the long run, you will have to pick the pro seller account anyway. It's better to just do it now.

Amazon really values its sellers and hence, it also gives you a free month whenever you first sign up as a pro seller. So, if you think that you don't need the pro seller pack you can downgrade to a simpler account after one month. Amazon does not charge you for the pro account till after the completion of the one-month. It's kind of like a free trial.

As soon as you sign up you also get the free Amazon seller app that you can use to scan products that you find at your home and at stores. The app is kind of like Scoutify except that it is free. If you are a starter then you should definitely use this app since it is simpler to use and you wouldn't be wasting any money.

Tools

There are certain tools that you will require if you want to be a fully-fledged seller. The first basic thing is a computer. If you don't have one, then you can't really become a seller. Your Smartphone can't replace your laptop. You need one to keep tabs of all the orders and to put up your products. Make sure that your laptop is well equipped because if you do decide to sell on a regular basis, it will become your best friend.

Secondly, you will need a Smartphone. There are thousands of apps out there that are really helpful for a seller. If you want to be an expert at what you are doing, then you need that phone so that you are always on the tip of your toes. It also allows you to be better at what you are doing. You can sell your products even if you are out on a vacation and you'll easily be able to upload photos and information about your product even if you're not at home.

You will need a shipping scale. A shipping scale measures the weight of your box. It's important because an increase in weight even by a few grams can cause a lot of problems. This tool will come in handy since your box won't get returned because of it being the wrong size.

A box sizer is important for anyone trying to save money. You can cut down a huge box to the size that you want. This allows your package to be more compact and you don't even have to put something in the filler space. This is a huge problem because packing fillers can take a lot of money. Cut down your box so that it easily fits the product.

Bundle stickers are also important. If you want to send a set to someone then Amazon might separate them. This can be a huge problem because sets have to go together. Bundle stickers tell Amazon that the products are in one set and need to stay together.

Self-sealing poly bags work like magic. If you have to quickly pack something then you can just throw them into self-sealing poly bags and they are ready to go. There are numerous products that can be easily and quickly packed using poly bags.

You can also buy a Dymo printer if you want to save your time. A Dymo printer saves a lot of ink because it is thermal and it also prints item labels on demand so you don't have to wait until the end in order to print the labels.

Dymo Labels are suitable for a Dymo printer. They are water resistant and have a really strong adhesive. This makes them durable.

You also have to buy a scanner. You can buy a Bluetooth one that connects to your computer without any wires. It saves a lot of time and can be carried around easily so that you can scan items while working.

You should also get a bundle of address labels so that the courier service can find the address easily.

Other than that, you need good printers and label makers for your packages. Make sure that you buy this stuff in bulk because you're going to need a lot of it.

Chapter 5: Details of FBA

There are various things to consider when you are selling a product through FBA. There are numerous details that impact your profitability and sales. So, if you're someone who is selling the product without any consideration to the details you will probably have a lot of problems. Consider these small things before you take up FBA scheme as part of your business.

Costs

FBA is not cheap and there are various costs associated with it. If you want to be an FBA seller there are certain charges that Amazon will take from you. This reduces your profit margin and hence, you have to consider the FBA cost before you set the price for the product that you are selling.

The main cost of selling on Amazon is certain percent of your sale. This is something that you have to pay. Amazon is providing you with an online market to sell your product and hence, it is only fair that it takes some money on every sale.

FBA charges are not common for everyone. They are different depending upon the product. The item weight determines shipping cost, handling fees is mostly stable and same for all the products, the picking and packing fees depends on the distance that the Amazon representative has to travel and the amount of material that is used to package the product and storage costs also depend on the amount of space that is covered by the product. This is why it is recommended to sell products that are small. It seriously reduces all of these charges. Larger products take a lot of space and generally require a lot of shipping and packaging charges. You can cut down on the picking up charges by taking the product to the Amazon storage facility yourself. But this is hardly possible for most people since most of the storage facilities are located far away from cities.

You can use the FBA calculator app to see if it would be profitable for you to use FBA. You can't really consider the price of comfort here. Amazon does all the work for you in FBA and therefore, lets you focus on growing your business. This is why it's hard to really calculate if you will profit from FBA or not.

You have to consider cost before you select a product for FBA. You are not being forced to sell all products under FBA. If you find out that you are not going to make any profit by selling a product under FBA, then go ahead and sell that product through MF.

Selling products in bulk usually reduces their cost. If you sell just one water bottle then obviously the cost of selling it through FBA will be too much but if you sell a bunch of bottles, the cost per bottle would be very low. Be smart when you're selling products through FBA. Be aware of the customer demands and don't charge a higher price just for the sake of FBA.

Labeling

When you are sending the product to the Amazon storage service you have to label the product. There are two options that Amazon offers to you for labeling. Both of these options are very different and need to be considered carefully since they impact your sales and profitability. FBA Labeled Inventory involves putting a label on every product that you send to Amazon. This way Amazon can keep track of individual products that you send under the FBA scheme.

FBA Sticker less Inventory involves not putting any label on the package at all. Amazon identifies your product and mingles it with other similar products that are to be sold under FBA. This requires less work since your product does not have to be labeled and also ensures faster shipping because the products can be processed faster in groups.

Try both the methods for different types of goods that you are selling. If you try both the methods you will be able to understand which is better. Both methods costs the same but at the same time one will be suitable for a certain kind of product and one for a certain kind of product. Since sticker less methods clubs products of similar type together you might want to use this method for extremely common products to ensure faster delivery. The labeled method is safer because it's pretty common to see mingling fraud. To ensure that your product is safe, you might want to use the labeled method. You should definitely use the labeled method for products that are expensive to make sure that they are handled with care.

You might also want to consider labeling charges in your profit margin before you pick on any one method for your products.

Product

This is one of the most important parameter when you are trying to set up your FBA business. You have to make sure that your product has certain qualities. You also have to deal with everything related to your product in order to sell it and make a profit.

Make sure that your product is in the range of $10-50. You do not want to go ahead and buy an expensive product because it makes it very risky. There are better chances of being successful through FBA if you sell a cheaper product. Try to go for a perishable product that does not have a lot of uses. This is because customers usually want such products at a faster rate and hence, they look for FBA sellers. Make sure that the product is not too huge or heavy. Since, you have to pay for the storage of the product, it's better to make sure that the product is light and hence, does not cut down on the profit margin.

Go through your competitors. See if any of them have any product that has a rank of less than 5000 in the bestseller category. There are a lot of products on Amazon so if your competitor has some that's in the bestseller category it's better to stay away from that field. Also, try to look for a product that doesn't break easily. You do not want to deal with the loss of even one product. It might impact your profit margins. Make sure that your products are packaged properly when you send them to Amazon.

Check out the reviews of a product that you are going to sell. If a product has a lot of reviews then stay away from it. You shouldn't get into a niche that is already dominated by a certain seller. If there are less than 50 reviews of a product on the first page then the market for that product is mostly open and you can definitely get more customers at a lower price.

If you are making a product then you shouldn't spend too much. The manufacturing costs should only be twenty five percent of the actual sale price of the product. This will ensure that you are able to cover the FBA and other miscellaneous costs and are still able to make a sizeable profit on all of your sales.

Chapter 6: The Procedure

If you want to sell a product through FBA then you have to follow a certain procedure. It's important to make sure that you go through this procedure and understand it completely before you begin selling. Prepare yourself according to this procedure and by the products that you might need in advance. Remember, you can never be too prepared.

Step 1: Give Amazon your Product

In this step, all you have to do is send your product to Amazon so that they can store it for you. You can send in an absolutely new product and even a slightly used product if you want.

Go to seller central. Seller Central can be found in your account and here you can upload your listings. Your listings are your products and this is how your products will turn up on the website.

Amazon will the approve all of your listing or part of it. Amazon has a team of specialists that make sure that only true and high quality products are sold on Amazon. If you're selling good quality products then you won't have any trouble getting approved by Amazon.

Amazon provides you with a PDF that you can print if you want a label or you can also use FBA's label service as an alternative. Then you have to ship the product to Amazon. Amazon provides you with discounted shipping but if you want to use your own carrier and ship the product yourself, then you can use that option as well.

Step 2: Storing your Product

In this step, Amazon receives your product at its fulfillment storing facility and then stores it for you. Amazon will then catalog your product and store in their inventory. Amazon has some great storage facilities where your products are taken care of and are ready to be sent in just a few minutes, whenever it is required.

First, Amazon will receive all of your products and then scan them so that it can keep a track of your products. It also sends you an instant message, informing you that the product has been received.

Amazon then works on storing your product. It checks your product and notes down all of its units. They check the weight, height and other dimensions to find an appropriate place to store your product. It also helps in fixing the cost for handling and storing charges for the product.

Amazon provides you with world-class services. They keep a track of their entire inventory using their sophisticated tracking system. If an order is placed for a product then Amazon is able to find that product quickly so that it can be sent out. They also send you updates about the processing procedure. The tracking system is very effective.

Step 3: Dealing with Orders

In this next step, a customer finds your product and then orders it. Your job is done as soon as you ship the product to Amazon. The order execution is done completely by Amazon and its warehouse service providers. Amazon fulfills the orders that are directly placed on its site and it even fulfills the orders that you request which are not from the website. So, if someone informally asks you for your product, you can ask Amazon to ship him or her the product.

All of your listings are ranked on the basis of price. The price does not include any shipping costs at all. This is because all FBA users have the opportunity to sell their products without any excessive shipping costs.

All FBA products that you sell are eligible for Prime. So, if a Prime customer buys the product, Amazon makes sure that the product is delivered in two days.

If you fulfillment order is not from Amazon then there would be extra shipping costs and the customer won't be eligible for Prime delivery. This is because Amazon provides certain offers only to users that order through the website.

Step 4: Sending out the Product

In the next step, Amazon picks up your product out of its inventory and then packages it properly. Packaging is done again because Amazon makes sure that the product is not harmed and reaches the customer intact.

Amazon first locates your product. The storage facilities of Amazon are all huge. There are numerous products there and yet, Amazon picks up your product in only a few minutes after the order has been received. They have an extremely high-speed web-to-warehouse system. The system keeps a track of all the products and as soon as an order is received, the system locates your product and sorts it out. This system also packs your product carefully.

Customers are also given the option of clubbing their orders for your product with other products fulfilled by Amazon.

Step 5: Shipping

In the last step, Amazon sends out your product so that the customer can receive it. There are numerous products that are shipped from the warehouse everyday and yet, Amazon keeps a tab on all of these orders and sends you updates regularly.

Amazon sends out the product based on the delivery system that was chosen by the customer. If the customer needed the product in one day then Amazon will accommodate that request. The system isn't perfect and sometimes people don't receive their products in one day but this is very rare.

Amazon also provides the customer with tracking information. The customer can login to his/her account and check out where their order is. Amazon also sends similar updates to the seller.

If the order was on the Amazon website, then the customer can contact them if they have any issues. Amazon provides customer care for you. You don't have to talk to the customer directly at all. If there are replacements then Amazon also handles that.

The procedure is really simply and each step tells you about how you can make money by using FBA. So, if you want to use FBA you can simply follow the next steps that have been given below.

Step 1: Go to the Manage Inventory page and there select a product that you would like to include as an FBA listing. You will checkboxes in the left column. Simply select them if you want to sell a product under FBA.

Step 2: Click on the Actions menu and then select Change to Fulfilled by Amazon.

Step 3: Now, on the next page click on the Convert button.

Step 4: Then follow the guidelines given to dispatch your products to Amazon.

Conclusion

Thank you again for purchasing this book!

I hope this book was able to help you to understand the FBA scheme. FBA can be really complex for a first time seller. If you are one then I hope that the book gave you plenty of information to get you started. There are various benefits that come with FBA but there are various problems as well. Make sure that you are smart in your workings and study everything carefully before you start with your very own FBA business. Keep yourself flexible and take advice from wherever you can get it.

The next step is to setup your very own seller account. Go ahead and sell as much as possible on Amazon. Remember to keep a check on your profit margins so that you are able to take complete advantage of the FBA scheme.

Good luck!

www.ingramcontent.com/pod-product-compliance
Lightning Source LLC
Chambersburg PA
CBHW071525210326
41597CB00018B/2894